MY KIND OF HEROES

MY KIND OF HEROES

Elmer Kelton

State House Press

State House Press
Signature Edition, 2004

Copyright 1995, Elmer Kelton
All Rights Reserved
Second Edition, 2004. New material added.

Library of Congress Cataloging-in-Publication Data

Kelton, Elmer.
   My kind of heroes : selected speeches / by Elmer Kelton
   p. cm.
   ISBN 1-880510-27-8 (First Edition)
      1. Kelton, Elmer. 2. Authors, American – 20th century – Biography.
3. Texas, West – Social life and customs. 4. Western series – Authorship.
5. Texas, West – In literature.
I. Title

   PS3563.A2932Z47 1994
   813'54 – dc20   94-38220

Printed in the United States of America

State House Press
McMurry University Box 637
Abilene, Texas 79697
(325) 793-4682

No part of this book may be reproduced in any form or by any means
without permission in writing from State House Press.

Printed in the United States of America

ISBN 1-880510-85-5 (Signature Edition)
10 9 8 7 6 5 4 3 2 1

Book Designed by Rosenbohm Graphic Design
Hat Illustration by Author

Contents

MY KIND OF HEROES

A Note on the Signature Edition

My Kind of Heroes was first published by State House Press in 1995 as a collection of four selected speeches by Elmer Kelton. This revised second edition, or Signature Edition, includes three of those pieces plus two others.

The title essay, "My Kind of Heroes," leads off this new collection. Also retained from the first edition are "Myth vs. Reality" and "Politically Correct or Historically Correct?"

For this keepsake edition, we added "The Truth of Fiction," in which Mr. Kelton discusses the influence of history and Western literature on his own writing, and "Oil Boom Days in West Texas." They replaced the piece on "Racial Relations in the Western" that was in the first book.

While all of these stories were delivered originally as speeches, some of them have been revised slightly so they would work better in print. We also tried to eliminate some of the duplication from one piece to another without altering the meaning or context of the individual essays.

As an author, Elmer Kelton has always been generous about autographing books for his thousands of fans. This time we asked him to put his signature right up front. In many ways, these speeches—these essays or stories—are his signature statement about many of the things he believes about the West, about writing, about history.

Glenn Dromgoole, Managing Editor
State House Press
Abilene, Texas

My Kind of Heroes

When I was a kid on a ranch in Crane and Upton counties, we had an old fellow whose job it was to take care of seventy some-odd windmills on the place.

He always had some story out of the past to top anything new that came up. He had always seen something bigger or smaller, better or worse. He had seen the grass taller or thinner, cattle higher or cheaper, whatever comparison he needed at the moment to make the strongest impression.

I remember once when we were in a long dry spell, and he declared, "I seen it like this before, and it ain't goin' to rain till this wind quits blowin'." A little later he said, "This wind ain't goin' to quit blowin' till it rains."

But I think the statement I always liked best was on the day he solemnly declared, "Things just ain't like they used to be. And I don't think they ever was."

Things on farms and ranches today *aren't* like they used to be. And in some ways they probably never were like the stories, or like people want to remember them or imagine that they were. For one thing, there probably never were any really "good old days" in the ranching and farming business.

Almost anybody can tell you his own version of the good old days. You'll usually find that they were when he was *young*, and not necessarily when the business was in a state of prosperity. Listen closely to the stories about the good old days, and you'll usually discover that people suffered a lot of hardships. Part of their pride in those good old days is that they survived.

Listen hard to an oldtimer's humorous stories about better days and you'll usually find there was a certain amount of pain and anxiety that seems a lot funnier now in the telling than it did when it happened.

Kathy Greenwood has written a book called *Heart Diamond* about her experiences as a girl growing up on a ranch near Roswell, New Mexico. In it she makes a point that the events which cowboys laugh hardest about are those that skirt right up to the edge of disaster but pull back at the last possible moment. Often as not they have to do with somebody's wreck on a horse that almost but not quite got him killed, or a cow or bull which came that close to putting a horn through somebody.

We have a habit of glamorizing the past and imagining that it was better than it was. It may have had its compensations, but it wasn't like the image we see when we look through the rose-colored glasses of a creative memory.

My grandfather, Bill Kelton, grew up around Baird and the Eula community of Callahan County. He had worked on ranches and had broken horses and mules ever since his own father had died when Granddad was barely past ten. Later he cowboyed from the lower Pecos River all the way up to the XIT Ranch before he married.

Times were tough in Callahan County about 1906. Granddad began to itch to go farther west, where he might find work. His brother, my great-uncle Frank, was punching cattle at Pecos and wrote home that there were cowboy jobs to be had.

Granddad wanted to go to Pecos, but Grandmother had heard how hard that Pecos country could be. She said she wouldn't go a mile farther west than Midland. Granddad declared that they were going to Pecos.

They got off the train at Midland. Granddad spent his first winter there as a drayman, hauling freight until he found a ranch job north of town.

In those days it was customary that when a ranch hired a family man it fed the family as part of the deal—one reason they worked so many bachelor cowboys. My grandparents by that time had five children.

Granddad worked a good while on this ranch until the rancher decided those kids had too big an appetite. He let Granddad go. Then he offered to hire him back provided he would work on a bachelor basis and feed his own kids. Times being what they were, he did it.

The odd thing is that he always considered that old man one of the best people he knew. I guess he respected a man who knew how to hold his money together. Most ranchers in that country couldn't do it.

My dad told me the history of a lot of the ranches and ranch operators in the Midland-Odessa country. He knew most of them and cowboyed for a lot of them in his youth. No matter how funny Dad's story was, it usually tended to end on a sad note. Invariably the rancher seemed to have gone broke eventually and lost it all. Dad would say, "That outfit went under in '22," or "the receivers took them over in '24." In one case, "He finally lost it all and went to work as a night watchman in Midland."

Sure, agriculture has seen some tough times in recent years. It was tough in Granddad's time, and Dad's. It has always been tough. With very few exceptions, the ones who managed to survive the hard knocks of the teens, '20s and '30s were the tight-fisted ones who never spent a nickel without squeezing it until the buffalo bawled and the Indian squalled.

The late Vic Pierce told me that the way the wealthy ranchers in the Ozona country put so much money together was they never spent any of it.

I heard an Oklahoma rancher tell a group one time that he never bought a new nail if he could straighten out a bent one.

Billy Peays was an oldtime wagonboss in the Midland country, and he sometimes did a little small-scale ranching of his own. He would save his wages until he got enough to lease a little acreage and buy a few cattle. Then he would ranch until he had used it all up.

Happy Smith was a cowboy in the Odessa country. He told me one time that he was day-working on an outfit with Billy Peays in the Crane County sandhills. There used to be a lot of arrowheads in that country because it had been a Comanche hunting ground. As the wind would shift the sand around, you would find arrowheads on the scoured-out hardpan.

One day while they were on drive, he saw Billy get off his horse and pick up something from one of those scoured spots. When they brought the herd together Happy wanted to see what Billy had found. It was just an old rusted bolt with two washers on it. The bolt was beyond salvation, but the washers were all right.

Billy said, "If you ever get a place of your own, you'll learn to pick up things like that."

Which reminds me of a story historian J. Evetts Haley told about a tightwad banker up on the plains a good while ago. This banker liked to keep a horse boarded out. For one reason or another he lost his arrangement and had to find a new place to keep the horse.

Most of the people shied away from doing business with him. They knew him too well. But there was a poor old boy at the edge of town who needed money, and he offered to board the banker's horse for twenty dollars a month.

The banker threw a fit. He hammered and wheedled until finally the poor fellow offered to keep the horse for fifteen dollars.

The banker shouted, "What do you think I've got over there, a money factory?" He kept hammering and browbeating until at last the guy out of sheer exhaustion and desperation agreed to take ten dollars to put up the horse.

Flushed with victory, the banker said, "And by the way, my wife has a flower garden. I'll expect to get the manure."

The poor fellow said, "Friend, at ten dollars a month, they ain't goin' to *be* no manure!"

That's the kind of atmosphere I grew up in, and I guess it's colored most of the things I've ever written, whether they were articles for the *Livestock Weekly* or fiction about old times and modern times. I've heard too many hard-time stories to believe life was ever *very* easy for *very* long.

Dad told me he remembered people who went broke on land they had bought on credit for a dollar an acre.

My great-uncle, Frank Kelton, once had a cow herd all but *given* to him during a long drought in the Pecos country. But his reserves were limited. The drought lasted about a week longer than he did. He finally had to turn the cows over to the bank a week before the rains started.

There was a lot of that in the "good old days." We tend to remember the romance and the *good* stories and forget the hard times that would give us a better perspective on our own.

For the average person, whether he worked for wages or operated a farm or ranch, the wolf was always at the door. The main difference between the little outfit and the big one was the size and number of the wolves.

Years ago, when the Snyder oil boom was at its height, I interviewed an old man who was then way up in his eighties. He told me, "Son, when I was a young feller I could've swapped a good pair of leather boots for a hundred acres of land right in the middle of that oilfield.

"And there I was ... *barefooted*."

The late Bob Johnston of San Angelo used to be a big-steer operator in the heyday of that trade. He told me his father was trailing cattle north soon after the Civil War. He settled on the Trinity River bottom not far from Dallas.

Once when Mr. Bob was young he was helping his father gather horses off of the river. His father told him that right after the war he could have bought the land where Dallas is today for a bit an acre. He said, "I just didn't have a bit."

Mr. Bob ran big steers in the Osage and the Flint Hills of Oklahoma and Kansas for more than twenty-five years. He broke even or lost money a lot more times than he ever came out with a big profit. But each year when it came time to buy back in, he said he could never remember anything but those years when everything had worked.

Only one time did he ever make what he considered "a big killing." That was in 1945. He decided that was his cue to retire from the big-steer business. He didn't figure he could wait another twenty-five.

I remember a story I heard back in the long 1950s drought, when people were trying real hard to find something to laugh about. It seems that in the 1930s depression an old boy lost his land but still had a little bunch of goats. He started herding them up and down the lanes in McCulloch and Menard counties, using the free grass in the rights-of-way.

He did this for months, until he was mortally sick of it. One day he rode up to a ranch house and made the rancher an offer. He said, "I'll flat *give* you those goats if you'll just take them off my hands and get me out of this lane."

The rancher looked them over and said, "I'll take them if you'll give me a ten percent cut."

Out of all the adversity over the years has come one thing that has always struck me about ranchers and farmers. That is their ability to laugh at their problems. When things are the roughest, and there's no light at the end of the tunnel except perhaps an oncoming train, most of them manage to keep a touch of humor.

Back in 1931 my dad was running a small bunch of cows of his own while he cowboyed for the McElroy Ranch Company. He was paying lease on a pasture the McElroy wasn't using. One day old Uncle Dodge Magee offered to buy his little bunch of steer yearlings.

Neither Dad nor Uncle Dodge had been to town in a while, and they didn't know the market had taken a big drop. They agreed on a price. While Dad gathered the steers, Uncle Dodge went to town and found out how bad the market really was.

Like most of those honest old-time ranchers, he stuck by his deal. He took that little bunch of steers even though they took a strip of his hide. He told my dad, "Buck, the only way I'll make those steers pay out is to break them to work!"

One time in the late 1970s the lamb market dropped twenty dollars in a few weeks' time. A little group of lamb feeders around Goldthwaite lost half a million dollars before they had time to realize what was happening to them.

Layton Black told me, "The buzzards have all left my sheep pens. They're roosting down at my house."

Even age doesn't always stop them.

Hugh Campbell of Ballinger was a veteran of the four-section homesteading days out in far West Texas, and in later years he ran registered Hereford cattle. When he was up close to ninety, he broke his leg. He had jumped on a mare and tried to head a cow back down a fence. The cow cut to one side, and the mare cut back after her, but Mr. Hugh didn't quite finish the turn. He wound up on the ground.

I visited him while he was recuperating. He told me, "I don't blame that little mare one bit. Wasn't her fault. I ought to've taken time to put a saddle on her."

There used to be an old black bronc rider in San Angelo named Albert Merrill. He was still breaking broncs up into his seventies. One of them finally threw him off, and Albert wound up in the hospital with a broken leg.

One of his friends said, "Albert, at your age don't you think it's time to quit trying to ride those old broncs?"

Albert said, "When a man has got a settin'-down job, he'd better hang onto it!"

For years Robert A. Halbert of Sonora was one of the nation's top breeders of Polled Hereford cattle. Once when he was in his eighties I found him mixing concrete and shoveling it into a form to build a water trough. He had several men standing there leaning on their shovels, but he didn't trust them to do it right.

Late in his life, Mr. Halbert started having heart problems, and they installed a pacemaker in his chest. Soon after he went home, his son-in-law Vestel Askew went by to see about him. He didn't find him, but he found one of the ranchhands and asked where Mister Halbert was.

"The *patrón*, he is out there, *por allá*, in the big pasture."

Vestal was horrified. "You mean he's out there with that pacemaker, driving around in his pickup?"

"Oh no, *señor*. He is just on his horse."

Despite all the hardships, despite all the economic pitfalls, most people who have lived the farm and ranch life seem to have enjoyed it. I've talked to a lot of old men who spent the major part of their lives doing something else, but for most of them the real high point was that time in their younger years when they worked as cowboys, or when they and the bank together owned some cows.

My grandfather and grandmother had a pretty tough time for most of their lives. I've told you how Granddad started. Eventually he spent fifteen years as foreman of the Five Wells Ranch north of Midland for the Scharbauer Cattle Company. During all those years my grandmother cooked for a crew of cowboys, anywhere from two or three men to a dozen or more. She never got paid for it. It was just a fringe benefit of being a foreman's wife.

The last twenty or so years of my granddad's life he owned a partnership in a small leased ranch north of Midland. He never made any big money, never even owned a pickup, but he finally knew a measure of comfort. The wolf wasn't at the back door anymore. It stayed out past the yard fence.

In the early 1940s, just before I went off to the service, Granddad sold out his ranch interests and bought a house in town. The older folks knew, but they didn't tell us youngsters until they had to, that Granddad had a terminal cancer.

Just before he left that old place, I walked into the barn. Granddad was in there, but he didn't see me.

He was engrossed in thought, and he had as sad a look on his face as I ever saw. He was standing there rubbing his old hands over his saddle.

Looking back on it after he died, I realized he was bidding goodbye to a way of life that had been rocky and rough, but it had been his life and he had loved it. He hated to give it up.

It's still that way. Most people farming and ranching today hope to make a living, of course, but there are almost certainly easier ways of doing that. They stay with it because they like it. That's why their fathers stayed with it, and their grandfathers.

It isn't always a good living, but it's a good way of life.

It's a way of life I've always enjoyed writing about. And the things I've seen, the stories I've heard, have often found their way into the stories and books I've written.

The Time It Never Rained is about the seven-year drought of the 1950s. It is a novel—fiction. But in a sense it is a true story, because just about everything in that book happened to somebody I knew or knew about. Essentially all I did was to consolidate all those things into one group of characters who stood for all the real farmers and ranchers I knew.

Growing up on a West Texas ranch, around a bunch of cowboys, I heard a wealth of stories as a boy. My father never wrote anything longer than a letter, but he was a great storyteller in the old oral tradition.

When he suffered the first of several strokes that finally ended his life, I spent a lot of days and nights sitting up with him in the hospital. I got him to retell a lot of those old stories he used to tell when I was a boy. Most of the time I had a little tape recorder with me, and I have those stories on about a dozen or so hours of tape.

Out of those stories came much of the background for a novel called *The Good Old Boys*, set in 1906 at a time when my father was a small boy. I borrowed a lot from him and from my grandparents for that book.

I guess knowing so many of those old stories, told by the people who lived them, has helped color the kind of fiction I write. I can't write about heroes seven feet tall and invincible. I write about people five feet eight and nervous.

To me those are the real heroes. They fight their battles a day at a time. They do the best they can think of, and if that doesn't work, they try something else.

Most of all, they hang on and endure.

To me they are the salt of the earth. They are the rancher and the farmer—like my great-grandparents —who came out of the East Texas piney woods in the 1870s with a covered wagon and a string of horses, and settled a homestead in Callahan County.

Like my granddad, who was a cowboy and small rancher all his life.

Like my father, who followed the same road.

I never did qualify, myself. Dad gave me every chance to learn to be a cowboy. I was probably the greatest failure of his life. I was always better at talking about it, and writing about it, than I ever was at *doing* it.

And maybe it's better that way. By writing about them I've been able to honor those people in my own way. Perhaps a few of my books will even outlive me and stay around to tell our grandchildren something about our unique heritage. I hope so.

Because these people—the farm and ranch people—are my idea of heroes—past, present and future.

Myth vs. Reality

I don't trust the word "myth." To me, "myth" has always meant something not quite real, not quite true. It bothers me when learned academics in their Eastern ivory towers write or speak about "the myth of the Old West" or "the myth of the cowboy." To me, this implies that they were never actually real.

It bothers me almost as much when they refer to the West in past tense, as if it no longer exists, or the cowboy as a figure from the past—if they concede that he ever existed at all.

My great-grandparents came out to Callahan County from the East Texas piney woods in the

1870s with a covered wagon and a string of horses. They lived the pioneer experience. It was no myth, and neither were they.

My grandfather, their first child, was born after they reached the Eula community. They had not yet had time to build a house; they were still living out of their wagon. A neighbor lady insisted that my great-grandmother move in with her as time for delivery came near. My grandfather might otherwise have been born in a covered wagon, which would have given me a lot to talk about. As it was, he was born in a log cabin. That's a pretty good pioneer image, too.

But it is not a myth, at least as I define myth. It's what happened. It's the way life was in those days.

My great-grandfather died when my grandfather was only about ten. Granddad had to quit school and go to work to help his mother support his three younger brothers and two baby sisters. He broke horses and mules for Scott & Robertson and took ranch work wherever he could find it. In his bachelor cowboy days he worked as far southwest as the lower Pecos River and as far north as the XIT. As long as he lived, he was a cowboy. My father, too, was a cowboy all his life.

Myths? Not to me, not as I define "myth." They were real. The work they did and the lives they led were very real.

And though I never did become much of a cowboy myself, I always wanted to. I tried to live up to my forebears' image. Growing up in a ranch family, I was with real cowboys every day of my life until I went off to the university. What they did, what they believed, the stories they told, the things they taught me exerted a strong influence over my life. They have been reflected directly or indirectly in everything I have written.

My father never had much faith in government programs. During the seven-year drought of the 1950s, he and the ranch company he worked for never participated in the drought relief programs. He never trusted them. He preferred to go his own way rather than become entangled and beholden to them. He was not alone. I knew a number of ranchmen who stayed out, or who finally participated only when forced to.

When I wrote *The Time It Never Rained*, I did not have to look very far for the essential elements that went into the main character, Charlie Flagg.

I have heard Charlie described as a mythical character representing old-fashioned ideals of rugged individualism and free enterprise. To me, there was nothing mythical about him. He was real.

I don't know just where we separate myth and image. Perhaps we don't. They may be essentially the same.

I think we would all agree that there is a widely accepted image of the Texan, outside of Texas. It persists in other parts of the world, certainly in Europe. Speak the word "Texas" and it conjures up an image of a cowboy on horseback with a desert mountain and an oil well behind him. And a saguaro cactus. How that saguaro got in there, I don't know. Arizona could probably sue.

Every few years we go to Europe to visit my wife's home country, Austria. Since the TV show *Dallas*, I have just about given up wearing a Texas hat over there. Little kids were following me around, calling me "J.R."

We Texans have an image. It is not always the one we would like, but sometimes perceptions are more important than facts, at least in the way they make people react to us.

Some years ago an elderly New Yorker moved down to San Angelo and set himself up as a real-estate agent. He was 110 percent New York—in his walk, his talk, his manner, his clothes. He made no discernible effort to fit the styles of West Texas.

After he had been in San Angelo a couple of years he won a contest. The prize was a trip to a convention in New York. He bought himself a broad-brimmed cowboy hat and a pair of fancy cowboy boots, and he went back to New York looking like his image of a true Texan.

The opposite was true of J.M. Shannon, who got his start fencing the outside perimeter of the XIT Ranch and eventually became a wealthy landowner and sheepman in San Angelo. Despite his money, he went around looking more like a tramp than a wealthy rancher. The story is told that a stranger mistook him for a panhandler and offered him a quarter to hold his horses.

Shannon held the horses. He said money is money, and you earn it wherever you can.

A friend once encountered him on a street in San Angelo and asked why he didn't dress in a manner more befitting his station in life.

Shannon said, "Why should I dress up? Everybody around here knows me."

He made a business trip to one of the big cities, Chicago or maybe St. Louis. He wore the same clothes he wore at home. A friend said, "Can't you at least dress up a little when you go to the city?"

Shannon replied, "Why should I dress up? Nobody around here knows me."

The New York real-estate man had the image, but not the reality. J.M. Shannon was reality.

We can easily trace many sources of this image. The cowboy as a "knight of the range" probably owes more than a little to Sir Walter Scott, and probably even to Beowulf. The tall tales of David Crockett were a prototype for the tall Texas tales which followed. Ned Buntline and fellow writers of "penny dreadfuls" in the latter part of the 1800s made twelve-foot-tall heroes out of such real-life people as Buffalo Bill and Wild Bill Hickok as well as fictional characters like Deadwood Dick. They also began molding the working cowboy into a version of the Knights of the Round Table.

Along came Owen Wister with his novel *The Virginian* to give the cowboy a certain amount of class while setting in concrete his image as tall, silent hero. Ever since Wister, it has been difficult for writers to stray far afield of that image. Readers want it. New York editors will allow only so much tampering with it.

Hollywood got on the bandwagon early. One of the first films to make a real impact on the public was a Western, *The Great Train Robbery*. Incidentally, it was made in New Jersey, and reflected the Eastern image of the Wild West.

Bronco Billy Anderson became the screen's first consistent Western hero. William S. Hart came along fairly early. His Westerns had a gritty, dusty, lived-in look, somewhat like the much later spaghetti Westerns. But the stories were much in the Owen Wister tradition. Hart was often the bad man with a good heart, tall and brave, redeemed by a good woman's love.

Tom Mix came along. His first short Westerns were often playful and had a lot of real cowboy in them. But after a while they got fancier, with a lot more action and glitz than Hart would ever tolerate, and the public ate them up. Hart and Bronco Billy went into eclipse. People liked this cowboy with the white hat that never got dirty and the beautiful horse that did everything but read the papers.

In one Fred Thomson silent Western, *Thundering Hoofs*, the horse even kneels in prayer at his master's grave.

The Western had become a morality play, the cowboy hero a role model for red-blooded American boys. The traditional cowboy hero was the personification of the Boy Scout motto.

A lot of the early cowboy movie actors came from the Wild West shows and rodeo. Flashy horsemanship and super-smart horses became a staple of the B Western.

My dad seldom went to the movies. So far as I know, he never saw but one or two Western films before he finally broke down and bought a television set in his later years. Even then he preferred Jackie Gleason or Ed Sullivan to *Gunsmoke*. Dad loved horses, but he had no illusions about their intelligence, or lack thereof. I used to wonder what he would have said if he had ever seen Ken Maynard's horse Tarzan race to untie Ken with his teeth and rescue him from a burning shack. He would probably have walked out of the theater.

Dad was aware of the image, but he never bought into it.

Hugh Campbell and his brother Seth had homesteaded out in the Kermit sandhills at the turn of the last century. He had cowboyed all over that Western country in his youth, and he remembered the resistance the four-section homesteaders received from some of the big ranchers.

Back in the early 1970s, Hugh went to a bull sale out in Arizona. Henry Elder, editor of the *Texas Hereford Magazine,* took a picture of him with John Wayne. Wayne stood about six feet five. Hugh was more like *five* feet five. In the picture, they reminded me a little of Mutt and Jeff.

Hugh admitted to John Wayne that he had never seen one of his movies. "I don't have to go to the picture show to see how it was," he said. "I was there."

John Wayne was the image. Hugh Campbell was reality.

Hugh once had a run-in with a famous gunfighter, Deacon Jim Miller, and his reaction was not quite like Wayne's would have been, at least the Wayne we saw in films. Hugh was helping ship cattle out from near Monahans once when a cow turned back and stuck a horn in his ribs. The doctor cleaned him up and sewed him up but wanted to keep him around a few days for observation, to be sure he didn't get blood poisoning.

The ranch placed Hugh in a boarding house by the railroad tracks. He was feeling awfully bad. The wound hurt. He was running a high fever and had a terrible headache.

This was at the time of the four-section home-steaders, who were taking up a lot of state land over West Texas. Some big ranchers in the sandhills hired Jim Miller to discourage as many homesteaders as he could. He had a reputation as a cold, hard killer, and the reputation was justified. He ran several home-steaders out, but one day he came upon a settler who didn't intend to leave and parted Miller's hair with a .30-.30 slug.

Hugh was trying his best to get some sleep, but somebody kept firing a pistol on the front porch. Hugh finally lost his temper and went downstairs. He saw a man with his head wrapped in a bandage, shooting birds off the telephone line that ran along the tracks. Hugh gave him a round cussing and told him if he didn't put up that pistol, he would give him a good whipping. Then he walked back inside and asked the landlady who that so-and-so was, doing all the shooting.

She said, "Don't you know Jim Miller?"

Hugh said he had a speedy recovery and went back to the ranch. He hadn't seen any John Wayne movies. He had no image to live up to. He was more interested in continuing to live.

Incidentally, Jim Miller got his come-uppance afterward in Oklahoma, at the hands of a lynch mob. They decorated the rafters of a barn with Miller and several other social misfits who had overstayed their welcome.

As a boy I loved to attend the Western movies when I got the chance. That was not often, because we lived nine miles from town. I used to marvel at the superb marksmanship of the movie cowboys. In the first of the long series of Hopalong Cassidy films, Hoppy, firing a six-shooter from horseback, shoots a gun from the villain's hand at a range of at least fifty yards. That was fiction—the image.

In real life, the McElroy Ranch had a chuckwagon cook who kept a six-shooter in the chuckbox. One day, one of the best cowboys I ever knew borrowed that pistol to kill a beef. At a range of about six feet—point-blank, you could say—I saw him miss three shots. He finally had to bring the beef down the old-fashioned way, with the back side of an ax. That was the reality.

If he hadn't been trying to live up to the image, of course, he would probably not have tried the six-shooter in the first place.

It is hard to define sharp lines between myth, image, tall tale, legend and folklore. To a large degree, perhaps, they are pretty much the same.

One of my favorite Texas tall tales was told by the late Stanley Frank, who published *Livestock Weekly* for forty-five years.

A group of ranchmen were drinking coffee in a café at Mertzon, and they got to talking about the great dogs they had. The first liar didn't have a chance. Each one in his turn topped all the other stories about the intelligence of their dogs. Sonnie Noelke was sitting and listening; he hadn't said anything.

The telephone rang, and the waitress told Sonnie he had a call. When he came back, somebody asked, "Who was it, Sonnie?"

Without cracking a smile, Sonnie replied, "Aw, it was just my old sheepdog. He said he has the lambs in the pen, and he wanted to be sure I didn't forget to bring the drench."

Oil Boom Days in West Texas

I grew up in the edge of the oilpatch, at Crane, in the Permian Basin. It was still in final throes of its boom phase in 1929 when we moved to the McElroy Ranch, where my dad got a cowboy job, then became a foreman and finally general manager.

Crane County's original discovery well was drilled in 1926 by wildcatter B.F. Weekley in a partnership with Church and Fields. Crane City was born the same year I was.

The history of that well was typical of so many wildcats elsewhere. Weekley was at the end of his string. His well was beginning to show all the signs of being a dry hole, and he wasn't sure he could pay his bills. He owed $500 to John Garlin, one of his drillers. He offered Garlin an offset eighty acres in lieu of the money. Garlin held out for the cash. After supper Weekley took his crew back to make one last run before dark, and maybe the last one ever. That run brought in the county's first oil well and started the Crane County boom.

The late Bill Allman told me that the offset eighty acres, offered to pay off a $500 debt, was sold shortly afterward for $80,000, a fortune in 1926.

All the stories weren't like that. Weekley owed $1,500 to a rig builder named Jones and talked him into taking a 160-acre lease in payment. Jones sold the lease for $100,000.

Weekley had two other wildcat wells drilling at the same time as his discovery well. They came in dry.

Most of the people who went to Crane in the early days were honest, hard-working folks just trying to make a living. But when the place was still a young tent city, the proprietor of a new cafe got into an argument with his cook. The cook stabbed him with an icepick. One of the witnesses said, "Guess we'd better carry him over the hill someplace and bury him." That was the origin of the Crane cemetery, which is still in use today.

A woman who was working in the cafe simply took it over and ran it for some years. She didn't have a deed, so far as anybody knew. Nobody cared much for such niceties in those days. Boomtowns tended to have a short life anyway. The "smart money" would have bet that the town wouldn't even be there in another six months.

For that reason, folks weren't in a hurry to build a jail. For a while, a heavy chain and a stout post served the purpose. Peace officers would handcuff a prisoner to the chain and leave him there to consider the error of his ways.

One of the early justices of the peace—a lady—had a rudimentary view of justice that would drive a modern-day ACLU lawyer straight up the wall. A couple of men were brought before her on a charge of fighting for the umpteenth time. She told them to take a pair of ax handles, go off into the brush where they wouldn't bother anybody, and beat each other to death.

I came across an account of a peculiar mishap while going through the old discarded McElroy Ranch correspondence files a few years ago. After the Franco-Wyoming Oil Company interests bought the ranch in 1926, they hired Lester S. Grant to come down from Boulder, Colorado, to manage both the ranch and the oil interests. He had spent many years mining in South America and was teaching at the Colorado School of Mines. He was just one of many who came out of mining into oil.

Before leaving Colorado he had bought a big retractable steel measuring tape to use in survey work. When the Crane townsite was carved out of the McElroy Ranch property, he and others used that tape to measure off the town lots.

They had most of the job done before somebody discovered that the tape had a flaw, several inches missing out of it. The lots had been laid out too short. By the time the surveyors had staked the whole townsite, the discrepancy had reached major proportions on the far side. They had to do the whole job over. I don't know if any buildings had to be moved. Most weren't very permanent anyway. A majority of the population lived in tents.

The few solid buildings could be jacked up onto skids.

My old teacher and mentor Paul Patterson said they called the town Crane City when it wasn't a city and shortened the name to Crane when it became a city.

I have some very sketchy memories of the town as it looked when we moved to the ranch in 1929. I was three-going-on-four. There were still a great many tents, some of them floored and boarded up on the sides. A lot of people lived in small houses with wooden framing and sheet-iron siding.

The "shotgun" style was popular. People said you could fire a shotgun through the front door, and the shot would go out the back door . . . if nobody was standing in the way. Of course, if no one was standing there, why would the shot have been fired in the first place?

One common fixture I can remember was the water barrel that stood in front of just about every house before the town put in its first water system. Men used to haul water by truck or wagon and deliver it to the door for a dollar a barrel.

When today's Texas water situation is discussed, you occasionally hear someone declare that someday water will be worth more than oil. I remember when it was. Oil was ten or twenty cents a barrel, but water was a dollar.

It was a financial tragedy for a family in those days when a stray horse or cow came along and nosed the cover off of one of those water barrels.

If your water got spoiled, you could drink soda pop for a nickle a bottle. I don't know what beer cost. That was a forbidden subject around our house, and a lot of other homes in Crane.

I vividly remember as a small boy watching from some distance as part of a tank farm burned between Crane and our camp house in the sandhills. Later on, when a preacher told us about the eternal fires of damnation, I had something to relate to.

Speaking of fires, I remember the flares that used to burn all over the oilfields, burning off gas. We called them "torches." The biggest one was north of town in the old Humble Camp. Over the years the pipe gradually melted down several feet from the top. It went out a time or two and gassed some people to death. I remember workers shooting flaming arrows up into the escaping gas to relight it.

They used to tell a story about a tramp who crawled into the open door of a freight car and went to sleep. He woke up as the train was passing through an oilfield. Seeing all those flares, he thought he had died and the jaws of hell had opened up to receive him.

Cattle used to bed down around these torches for warmth in the winter. They were forever drinking oil out of the open pits, too. There was something about the smell of oil that attracted them, some mineral deficiency that led them to lick it or drink it. If they got enough of it, they died right there, or close by. More often, they just went into a long, general decline. They would get as poor as snakes and usually had to be shipped for salvage. An oiled cow seldom recovered completely.

Oilmen used to say that there was nothing so good for the cattle market as getting a cow killed in the oilfield. She might have been an old cull before, but she was a high-priced registered animal when the claim went in to the oil company.

The McElroy Ranch was deeply involved in the oil business itself, so it never played that game. It had a standard set of damage prices that reflected realistic values.

A number of old burned-out cars and trucks were scattered over the ranch, relics left over from the early oil-boom days when the roads were nothing much more than sand pits. A car or truck would get stuck in the sand, and the driver would burn the engine up trying to force his way out. Most of those old hulks were picked up during the scrap-metal drives of World War II.

The fathers of most of the kids I went to school with were involved directly or indirectly with the oilfields. The population was highly mobile in the exploration and development stage. An oilfield would get a lot more stable once the production stage became dominant over exploration.

In those days Crane was strictly a workers' town. Oil-company executives lived in Midland, or Fort Worth or Dallas. Everybody close to the patch was on a somewhat equal economic level.

Hardly anybody there, including the merchants, was more than two or three paces ahead of the wolf. In those Depression days the amount of your salary was not the first consideration. Having a salary, having a job was reason enough to be grateful.

I recall seeing an old bus once that had been converted into a crude version of what might later be called a mobile home, with a kerosene stove and bunks that folded up. It offered a home—such as it was—for a family who moved often. As a boy, I thought it was a neat idea and a fun way to live, carrying your house with you from one oilfield to another. I didn't realize what a symbol of hardship it really was. Now, when young people ask me about the Depression, the image of that bus comes to mind.

The fact that there was no one to envy gave Crane and oilpatch towns like it a sense of equality, of fellowship that might be hard to find in most other situations. Nobody had any reason to feel superior, or inferior. There was a feeling that we're all in this together.

Anybody's good fortune was everybody's good fortune, and anybody's bad luck was shared—in spirit, anyway—by everybody. That spirit seemed to prevail in most of the oil towns in those times. It still does.

I have a lot of good memories of those oilpatch days of the 1930s. At the time, as kids, we didn't fully appreciate the problems the Depression was giving our parents. Nobody had much money, so nobody expected a lot. We didn't see many people better off, so we didn't feel put upon or discriminated against.

We took a lot of pleasure from small things. An ice-cream cone once or twice a week was a real treat. They were a nickel. You didn't get a nickel every day to throw around. A big candy bar was a nickel, too, the kind you find today for fifty cents, if you're lucky.

We didn't have a school cafeteria in those days, so everybody packed a lunch or brought lunch money. There were a couple of little cafes near the school ground which charged fifteen to twenty-five cents for a plate lunch. Twenty-five cents was exorbitant for school kids, but some of the hard-working oil-field roughnecks could eat enough to make it worth their while.

Pat Passur had a domino hall and a hamburger joint, separated by a partition. School kids were welcome into the hamburger side, but they were forbidden to stick their heads in the other side, much less to go in. He had his grill in the front window where you could stand outside and watch him make his hamburgers. They were the best in the world. I can still taste them. Today's quick-stops aren't even in the running.

They cost a dime. An old man set up a competing hamburger joint down closer to the school and sold his for a nickel apiece. They weren't as good as Pat's, but you got twice as much for your money.

I've been fighting that quantity vs. quality game ever since.

As kids, we saw mostly the positive side of the oilpatch and the town. We were dimly aware that a red light district existed, but we weren't quite sure what people did over there. We just knew that the preachers were against it.

We knew there was a certain amount of random violence, usually just roustabouts drinking too much and talking too much and getting themselves into fist fights. Murder was almost unheard of during the years I knew Crane best.

It was spared the kind of organized vice and vio- lence that beset some of the other boomtowns of the time. We used to hear wicked stories about places like Wink, where a well-organized gang more or less ran the town to suit themselves. The same sort of thing had happened in Borger, up in the Panhandle, until it reached a point that martial law was declared and the Rangers moved in.

The Rangers never had to worry much about Crane. They came in one time and broke up some slot machines, and they were always on the lookout for bootleggers.

Rangers stood out like a tall mountain against the sandhills. You could tell one a block away just by the way he carried himself, and by the pistol high on his hip. They were awe-inspiring. They looked like the cowboy heroes in the movies.

My dad once came across a bootlegger's stash in the brush when he was out working cattle. Just to see what would happen, he moved it. According to Bill Allman, two local bootleggers got into a pretty good fight shortly afterward. One thought the other had stolen his goods.

Nobody cared much what bootleggers did to one another. They were—or seemed to be—a pretty scruffy lot.

One of the early Crane sheriffs used to confiscate bootleg whisky, but he didn't pour it all out. An old-timer told me he served on a jury once, and the sheriff offered him a drink out of some contraband he kept beneath his desk. He said it was the worst stuff he had ever put in his mouth.

The people who followed the first boom into the sandhills of Crane County had to put up with a lot of hardship. Living accommodations were not very good. The houses tended to be flimsy and leaked wind, if not rain.

Our houses on the McElroy Ranch were better-built than most of those in the oilfields, but they weren't exactly luxury condominiums. A north wind would cause the window curtains to billow even though the windows were closed.

Dad said, "There's one advantage. Nobody was ever asphyxiated in a McElroy house."

Washing and drying clothes during a dust storm was a lesson in futility and frustration. We had a lot of dust storms.

I had all these memories, but for one reason or another I had long resisted the idea of writing a novel about early oilpatch days. The main reason probably was that even though I had lived in that environment, I never had actually worked in the oilfields myself. I didn't think I knew enough detail to write a believable story.

The nearest I ever came was a short-term job on a tanking crew one summer before I went into the service. It was the hottest, hardest, meanest work I ever did in my life. It reinforced my decision that I wanted to be a writer.

Since in a way I was always an outsider, I decided to write from the viewpoint of outsiders. I built the story around two main characters. One is a young cowboy who goes to the fictional oilpatch town of Caprock for a ranch job. It falls through, and in desperation he goes to work in the oilfield.

The other is the town sheriff. He has been sheriff when the place was a sleepy little cowtown about two blocks long and two blocks wide. Now, suddenly, he is trying to enforce the law in a place where the population has swelled into thousands. He just wishes the boom would bust and go away.

The story, *Honor at Daybreak*, tells about a lot of the people you would find in those early boomtowns: the independent wildcatter, skirting the edge of bankruptcy with an old standard cabletool rig; his friend and rival who seems to hit a gusher every time with his modern rotary outfit; the town bootlegger, who used to be a preacher and can quote the

Bible chapter and verse; the shooter, who hauls nitroglycerin around in the back of a converted Studebaker; a madam who runs the most prosperous business institution in town; and a woman, suggested by my own grandmother, who operates a ramshackled rooming house for oilfield workers.

Another element which plays a part in my story is one which Crane somehow avoided, but a lot of other early boomtowns did not. That is the organized criminals who moved in to take advantage of the loose money floating around.

I did a lot of research, some at the Permian Basin Petroleum Museum in Midland. I went to Lovington, New Mexico, and had a nice visit with Bill Allman, a family friend as far back as I can remember. He was an old-time cable tool driller, coming out of Kansas in the 1920s and staying with a cable tool outfit until he retired. He walked me through the cable tool operation, step by step, so that part of my story would be as realistic as I could make it.

He was ninety-two, and his mind was still as sharp as it had ever been. Every other year, when Odessa had its oil show, he would be at the cable tool rig there, showing visitors how it worked. He would stand out in that hot sun all day because he loved it so. The last time he did it, he was ninety-one.

He passed away a few months after my visit. He was still sprightly and bright almost to the hour of his death. I dedicated the book to him, and to two of my uncles who spent their working lives on a drilling platform.

I found several books that were helpful. I was not looking so much for the overall history of the oil industry as the daily lives and the working techniques of the people in it. Two useful books were *Tales from the Derrick Floor* and *Folklore of the Oil Industry*. Both were written by Mody Boatright, who taught me in a folklore class at the University of Texas in the 1940s.

Two more were *Voices From the Oil Fields*, by Lambert and Franks, and *Roughnecks, Drillers and Toolpushers*, by Gerald Lynch. Roger and Diane Olien, a husband-and-wife team in Odessa, have written several excellent books about the oilpatch and oilfield towns.

There are worlds of good stories to be found in the oilfields. The surface has barely been scratched. For many of these stories, it is too late; the people have passed on, especially those of the early booms.

I don't know what the future of the oil industry is. None of us do. But I do know it has a great history. I just wish more of it had been preserved, because we'll never see the likes of it again.

The Truth of Fiction

As a youngster I was an avid reader. I read everything I could get my hands on, even to the labels on cans of coffee and pork and beans.

The first book I ever owned was *Treasure Island*. Our teacher began reading it to us in the daily reading hour, and I got so caught up in it that I couldn't wait to see how the story came out. I badgered my mother into buying a copy for me from the Sears catalog at the unholy price of forty-nine cents, in hardcover. I still have the book.

We had a fairly small library in the Crane schools. I devoured it. I read all the standard childhood classics: *Tom Sawyer*, *Huckleberry Finn*, *Hans Brinker*, *Gulliver's Travels*. I have to concede that *Gulliver's Travels* was a little over my head. The thought of raising Irish babies to be eaten by wealthy English appalled me. Not until much later did I understand that Swift was using ironic fiction to illustrate a truth.

Though I read a variety of subject matter, what I always liked best was material about Texas and the West. I related to that, because it reflected the life I saw around me every day. I grew up on a ranch, where my father was the foreman. I was around cowboys all the time. I listened to their stories and absorbed the folklore of the range like a sponge.

I was spellbound by J. Frank Dobie, the great Texas folklorist. His book *The Longhorns* gave me a feeling for the oldtime cattle industry and the cowboy that stays with me to this day.

Nearly all my relatives on my father's side of the family were cattle people—cowboys and ranchers. I realized very early in my life that there was something different about them. On my mother's side, the men worked in the oilfields, so that kind of life was also part of my early experience.

As a boy I read and loved the great horse stories by Will James, such as *Smoky, Sand* and *Scorpion*. These never made any pretense at being anything other than fiction, though they reflected a lifestyle the author knew extremely well. They reflected a reality, at least as that reality was seen through Mr. James' rose-tinted glasses. Will James added another dimension to the cowboys I had known all my life.

Still another book in the school library taught me a great deal about cow people. It was Paul I. Wellman's *The Trampling Herd*, a non-fiction history of the American cattle industry from the time of Columbus' second voyage, though the era of the great cattle drives to Kansas, and to the end of the open-range period.

I read other great writers, fiction and non-fiction, on the subject, including Charlie Siringo, Eugene Manlove Rhodes and Stewart Edward White.

I won't try to kid you that all my reading was on this high plane. I once knew the plot of every book Zane Grey wrote. I used to wait until the corner drugstore tore the covers off of the previous week's *Wild West Weekly* and sent them in for a rebate; then I could buy the magazine for a nickel instead of a dime. I was thoroughly familiar with Walt Coburn, William Colt McDonald, Max Brand and other pulp writers of the day.

There is no telling how many hundreds of hours I spent reading material the teachers dismissed as "trash." But I don't begrudge one minute of it today. I don't believe any of it was really wasted.

Number one, it taught me to read, and to *love* reading.

Number two, it fired my imagination.

Number three, whatever its merits or demerits in the manner in which it reflected history, it gave me a deep and abiding interest in *real* history, an interest I might never have acquired had I devoted myself strictly to formal history and to materials my teachers considered "good literature."

Because I loved so much to *read* fiction, it was natural that I turned to trying to write it. I started at an early age, often writing stories at times when I was supposed to be studying other subjects.

English was always my long suit. I won most of the spelling bees and none of the football games. I turned in compositions that had not been assigned.

This was a time when, in an oil-patch town like Crane, a boy who excelled in English and won spelling bees was automatically suspect.

All those grand stories by Dobie and James and Grey would run through my head and fire me up to write stories of my own, out of my imagination. I couldn't get fired up over compound fractions and carrying *pi* to the fourth power. There were books in the library I hadn't read yet, and arithmetic was an unwelcome distraction that kept me away from them.

As I got older I became more selective about what I read. I became more critical. In the field of the Western I learned that some writers did honest stories with both feet firmly planted on facts, while others didn't know whether cows slept in caves or roosted in trees.

I think my first serious entry into the Western field as a writer was done with something of a missionary zeal. I knew that the history of the West was more than just a bunch of people running their horses around aimlessly over the prairie and firing off their pistols.

I knew that the typical cowboy was not a two-gun hero eight feet tall who spent his time protecting helpless schoolmarms or bosses' daughters from bearded villains who rustled cattle for a living and headquartered down at the Golden Nugget Saloon.

I wanted to write about the cowboy as I had known him, augmented by the background I had learned from Dr. Dobie, Will James and other writers I respected.

But I soon found that the public saw the Western basically as a story of action, of movement. There was little interest in a cowboy who took his problems to the courthouse. Unless, that is, he had to walk over an opponent to get there. Without action, Western stories wouldn't get printed. If printed, they wouldn't get read.

But I found there was a way to work action into these stories without doing injustice to history. There was, as we all know, a lot of violence in the real Old West, though not as much as Hollywood would lead us to believe. Some was plain outlawry, often with no motivation other than the fast buck, obtained without work. But much of it was honest conflict born out of opposing interests.

The rancher-homesteader clashes are a classic example, even though they have become a cliché from overuse. Each side was firmly convinced that it had a rightful case.

I found that throughout the history of the West there were always critical points of change, times and places where an established order was being challenged by something new. These changes seldom came easily. Often they were accompanied by violent confrontations . . . not necessarily the good guy against the bad guy, the white hat against the black, but honest men against honest men, each convinced he was right and probably sure that God was on his side.

Sometimes the conflict was not so much man against man but simply man against change, or man against nature.

I always liked to find these times in history and use them as the basis for a fictional story. That way I could work up a certain sympathy for both sides. In a simple black hat-white hat story, the reader knows exactly where his sympathies lie, and he has read enough stories or seen enough movies to know how the story is going to end.

But what if he cares something for both sides? What if he's not sure the hero has all the right on his side? What if he roots for the hero but can have some empathy for the hero's adversary and hates to see him lose? What if his loyalties are torn between the two opposing viewpoints, and he's not even sure how he *wants* the story to come out?

I've always liked, when I could, to let my story grow out of history. Some writers dream up a plot idea, then decide whether to set it in biblical times, or in the Old West, or perhaps in a modern Mafia family. For some of them, it works.

But to me, a real historical novel needs to be so tied to its background that it would be very difficult to lift it bodily and put it in another time and place. Its roots are too deep to transplant.

Some examples come to mind out of my own work:

Many years ago I decided to write a novel based on the Texas revolution against Mexico. I wanted to use real historical incidents, though my main characters would be fictional to give me the freedom to unfold the story as I wanted it. I chose an incident I did not feel had already been written to death: the massacre at Goliad.

I had no real villains in the story. To provide dramatic conflict I used two sets of brothers, one set

coming into Texas from Tennessee, the other set
native Texas Mexicans. Each of the brothers had a
vastly different viewpoint than his sibling. Through
their eyes I tried to show the elements which gradually built up to a war between two tragically different cultures.

One brother in each pair represented the "dove"
sentiment, and the other was a "hawk" when it came
to the conflicts that arose between American immi-
grants and the Mexicans. One of the Tennessee
brothers dies in the massacre at Goliad, and one of
the Mexican brothers dies in the decisive battle of
San Jacinto which won Texas independence from
Mexico.

The point I am trying to make is that this story,
published as *Massacre at Goliad*, could not be lifted
up and put in some other time and place without
radical surgery. It is rooted in one time, one place.

The background is factual. The story and the
characters are fiction. What I wrote never really happened. But it *could* have. Perhaps as J. Frank Dobie
was known to have said about some of his folklore
tales, if it didn't really happen that way, it *should*
have.

I would like to think that some people get interested enough after reading one of my fictional novels that they seek out the *real* history. Sometimes the fiction writer can help arouse interest in a neglected subject. Before *Jaws*, how many people were reading books about the great white shark? Before the movie *Titanic*, how many people were reading books about the *real* shipwreck?

Often, fiction is what shapes our perceptions of events, places and things. What we know—or think we know—about the age of chivalry, we have derived largely from the works of Sir Walter Scott. Our perception of the Southern home front during and after the Civil War is heavily based on *Gone With the Wind*.

Fiction is not necessarily an idle pastime. For years I kept thinking that the cowboy strike of 1883 at Tascosa, Texas, would make a good background for a novel. That strike reflected changing times, changing social values. It reflected the decline of the open-range West and its free and easy ways. It was an outgrowth, to a large extent, of the encroachment of the Industrial Revolution and the Eastern and European banking-and-factory mentality upon the range cattle industry.

It reflected the fencing-in of the cowboy, and the attempt to make him just another clock-punching hired hand. Except that he didn't and couldn't work by the clock—he worked by the sun, from *can* to *can't*.

The open range was clearly doomed by history, but there were aspects to its way of life that were hard to give up. The cowboy resisted. His resistance was futile, but it is to his credit that he tried.

As usual I used fictional characters to give me freedom. I compressed the time element for dramatic purposes. But though the story was fictional, I tried to stick to real history in all the major aspects. The story has some unlikeable people but no clear-cut villains and no clear-cut heroes. It has no big shooting scrapes.

I tried to show, through my characters, the typical life of the plains cowboy of that day, his reaction to social and economic change, and the gradual shifting of political and economic power in that region to a new order.

A fiction writer may sometimes use real-life situations and stories to his or her advantage.

In real life, the cowboys lost the strike. Some left that part of the country. Others stayed and agitated the big ranchers by taking up homesteads on lands the ranchers had been using. And some, to be frank about it, took up cattle stealing. So the ranchers hired Pat Garrett to bring about what they regarded as law and order. By this time he was famous for having killed Billy the Kid. The ranchers figured all he had to do was ride around over the country, visit the "undesirables," and many of them would decide the climate elsewhere would be better for their health.

I used the Garrett image but not the name. I made my gunfighter an older man, a relic of another time, just as the free-range cowboys themselves had become relics of another time. But somehow I never could quite bring him to life. He remained a flat, one-dimensional figure.

One day I was interviewing an elderly ranch-woman named Rachal Bingham at Spur, Texas. She told me a story about a man named Pink Higgins, noted in his time as a "shootist," a gunfighter who hired out his gun but managed usually to stay within the letter of the law, if not its spirit.

He was a man well into middle age and a friend of her father when Rachal Bingham was a young bride married to a cowboy named Al Bingham on the Spur Ranch.

The Spur and other ranches were losing cattle to thieves, and they hired Pink Higgins to stop it. One day, riding along a ranch road, he met one of the men he had accused of being a thief. They drew guns, and the cowboy came out second best. He was buried near where he fell.

A wooden head board was put up over his grave. Cattle would trample the mound and rub against the head board until it fell. One day, on his own, Al Bingham decided to put a fence around the grave to protect it. He loaded a wagon with posts and lumber and set off down the road. Presently, who should he run into but Pink Higgins himself?

Higgins asked, "What are you up to, Al?"

Bingham was in a cold sweat, but he told him. The old gunfighter rubbed his chin a minute, then said, "That's a good idea. I'll go help you."

So this tough old man helped build a fence to protect the grave of a man he himself had killed.

To me that was a wonderful story, and it gave me what I needed to bring my gunfighter character to life as a human being. I interpolated the incident into my story. Somehow my character became a real person to me after that, a tragic and lonely person. I really cared, then, what happened to him. At the end of the book, when he rides off to die in some distant place, a man who has outlived his own time and doesn't know it, I felt for him. He had become as real as if I had actually known him.

Now, some might question whether Mrs. Bingham's story was history or folklore. More than likely time had imbued it with some elements of her own, which to me makes it folklore. But it fit very nicely into fiction. And it had the ring of truth.

Neither the ranches nor the cowboys really won the strike, either in real life or in my fictional version. The cowboys were the immediate losers, but in the longer-range sense the big ranchers as a whole were doomed to pass out of the picture just as the open-range cowboys did. Many of the striking cowboys remained in the region and helped build towns and small farming communities. In time these took the political dominance away from the few big ranches and contributed to their eventual breakup.

Though the primary purpose of fiction has to be to entertain, it can also illuminate and explain.

Anybody who reads *The Day the Cowboys Quit* learns a little history whether he intended to or not—at least history as I interpret it—and even a little sociology, whether he intended to or not.

The book of mine which has attracted the most attention over time is either contemporary or historical, depending upon your age.

At the time I first wrote it, it was still contemporary. By the time it had been rewritten twice and finally saw print, it was historical, at least to my own children's and grandchildren's generation.

Aside from World War II, the most traumatic experience of my life was a seven-year drouth which West Texas suffered in the 1950s. Even while it was still in progress, I knew I wanted to use it as the basis for a novel. The drouth finally broke in 1957, and I started writing the first version.

It bounced like a bad check. I wrote it again, from page one, and it bounced just as high and far. So I put it away for about ten years and went on writing more conventional Western novels. By the early 1970s I had gained a lot more experience as a writer. Doubleday bought the third version and brought it out as *The Time It Never Rained*.

I told the story through the eyes of a proud middle-aged Texas rancher named Charlie Flagg, who watches the world changing around him and doesn't know quite how to contend with it. When the terrible drouth sets in, he fights to keep his dignity and independence, *and* his pride. Because of a stern heritage of self-reliance, he refuses to accept government aid. This costs him some of his friends, much of his land, and eventually even estranges his son, who is of another generation and sees nothing wrong with taking anything the government offers to give him.

I knew several real Charlie Flaggs in those days. Some of them became unpopular at the time, possibly because they were like a nagging conscience to others whose personal code was more flexible. But in recent years a lot of people have taken a fresh new look at government programs, and they're wondering.

I didn't have to do a lot of historical research on Charlie Flagg. I wrote the book out of lessons I grew up with; out of my observations as an agricultural reporter among my farm and ranch friends during those awful seven years; and among members of my own family, including my father, who suffered along with Charlie Flagg.

There is a lot of both history and folklore in the book. The things which happened to Charlie in my story happened to people I knew or heard about. In that respect, Charlie Flagg is fiction, but he is also fact, and folklore. And through him, I tried to show the truth of farmers' and ranchers' eternal struggle to survive against many adversities.

At the end of the story, Charlie is left with little in the way of material things, but he has hope—and he has kept his pride and his dignity.

The history of this country is the story of people who had very little *except* hope. On the basis of that hope they built for us the country we have today, with all its faults and all its virtues.

As a writer, using the medium of fiction to illuminate truth, I keep trying to tell that story over and over again.

Politically Correct or Historically Correct?

Theoretically, history should be locked in concrete. The things that happened *happened*, and that should be *that*. But, of course, it doesn't work that way. If two people witness a fender-bender from opposite sides of the street, they see and remember the incident differently. Historical events very often were seen in different ways by the people who witnessed them, so later historians have to pick their way through a minefield of ambiguities and contradictions.

Moreover, interpretations of history mutate as the years go by and the fashions change. Today we often see *historical* correctness take a back seat to *political* correctness.

In earlier times, writers, including historians, as well as the general public, tended to glorify the history of the West—of Texas—the accomplishments of our forebears. Today it has become much more fashionable to condemn Granddad and Great-Granddad for a multitude of sins, real or assumed.

In an earlier time, we were looking for heroes. It is a mark of today's deep-seated cynicism that we tend more often now to look for villains. We seem to find them in the same places, and in the same people, where we used to find heroes.

Some time back, I was talking to a group of students at Angelo State University. One asked me why most of my novels are set in history. The past is gone, she said. History is about dead people. Why should history mean anything to us, living today?

I told her that our everyday lives are rooted in history. We are all products of what has gone before. We live where we live because of things that have happened in our past and to those who preceded us.

The way we live, the things we believe in, are all rooted in the times, the beliefs, the histories of our parents, our grandparents, and many, many generations before them.

History is part of the present *and* the future. It is ongoing. There is a continuity between yesterday and today and tomorrow. If we are to understand what is happening around us today, and, just as important, to have any valid vision of tomorrow, we have to understand yesterday. We have to know our history.

Mark Twain once declared that history is a lie, agreed upon. The problem is that historians today don't agree upon very much.

We have a class of revisionists—historians *and* other writers—who have taken the history we used to agree upon and stood it on its head. They have sought villains where we used to seek heroes. And they have found them in Granddad—in our Euroamerican ancestors.

There *is* a dark side to our history. All of it was not written in the light. But those who see it only in terms of the warts are as one-sided as those who see only the glory.

I have no quarrel with those who say that we need to make Western history broader. I agree with observers like Patricia Limerick when they say that in the past we have often not given sufficient attention to racial and ethnic minorities. As a boy I was an avid reader of Western history. I read a lot about Custer and other famous frontier cavalrymen. I don't remember at that time ever reading that two whole regiments of that cavalry, as well as two regiments of frontier infantry, were black.

Because my forebears were Confederate, I read with a great deal of interest about the exploits of Texas Confederate soldiers. However, not until the University of Texas Press published the memoirs of Rip Ford many years later, and after Tom Lea wrote his monumental history of the King Ranch, was I aware of Colonel Santos Benavides and his unit of Texas-Mexican Confederate troops who harassed Union soldiers along the Texas-Mexico border.

Somehow these people were left out of the history books I read when I was a boy. So I have no quarrel with those writers who would include them in a broadened view of history today. It is high time.

I don't remember during my youth reading a great deal about the contribution of women in the history of the West, though there were already a number of books around had they been called to my attention. Sallie Reynolds Matthews' *Interwoven* was there; I just didn't know about it. I *did* read Agnes Morley Cleaveland's *No Life for a Lady* in the Crane High School library, and Zane Grey's novel about his pioneer ancestor, Betty Zane. The women were not entirely overlooked; you just had to hunt harder to find them.

I loved to read Western novels, which presumably were an exclusively male province. One author I liked was B.M. Bower, who wrote *Chip of the Flying U* and other early Westerns. Nobody told me at the time that the "B" stood for Bertha.

Fortunately, women and ethnic minorities have come in for much more attention by writers in recent decades.

Leckie's *The Buffalo Soldiers* has done much to illuminate the role of the black soldier. I have read several books in recent years about the black cowboy, including the prototype of these by Durham and Jones. I strongly recommend to you the black folktales of J. Mason Brewer and C.C. White's *No Quittin' Sense*, all in the East Texas tradition.

Past omissions continue to be corrected. The literature is there now if we choose to seek it out. And some of these books are by no means new. They have been out there a long time for those who wanted to find them.

Frank Linderman's biography of Pretty-Shield, the Crow medicine woman, has been around since 1932, and you can still get it today from the University of Nebraska Press. Others in this vein include Elaine Goodale Eastman's *Sister to the Sioux* and Kay Bennett's *Kaibah*, about her Navajo girlhood.

So perhaps the past omissions have been less severe than some of today's revisionists would tell us as they try to load us up with guilt.

And guilt is what they are peddling. But they are selective in placing their blame. They would put all of it on our white male ancestors of European origin or ancestry. They seem blind to fault in anyone else.

I do not intend to paint our forebears as plaster saints. They were not. They were human beings with the same human virtues and faults that we share today. They were no better and no worse than we.

What I *do* want is to see us regain a sense of balance in viewing our history, in contrast to the narrow, one-sided, guilt-ridden revisionist view we have so often witnessed in recent times.

True, many past writers in glorifying the early Western experience glossed over the hardships suffered by the pioneers, and they often did not acknowledge that each gain made by the newcomers meant a loss to the people who were already there.

For the average person who went west in the 1800s, life was hard, and it never softened up much. The reality fell far short of the dream. Glamour and romance were in the eyes of later beholders. An old-timer once declared, "I'm not one who longs for the 'good old days.' I was there."

It is true that the Old West had a goodly share of the misfits, the outlaws, the exploiters and out-and-out psychopaths. This kind has always tended to gravitate toward those places which have the least law enforcement; they still do.

I have never forgotten what an oldtime farmer and railroad man named Henry Moore told me once. He had witnessed the latter days of West Texas settlement. He resented the fact that the gunfighters and outlaws of the Old West had always received so much attention. He said those people were never anything more than the freaks in the sideshow.

To him the main event—the real heroes and heroines—were the farmers and ranchers, the cowboys and sheepherders, the freighters and railroad men, the carpenters and blacksmiths, the teachers and homemakers. Those people were the *builders*, he said.

They were not the greedy, grasping opportunists some of today's revisionists would paint them. They were mostly honest, hard-working people trying to survive against the longest of odds, the most grueling of hardships, trying to improve the little they had and build something better for their children. Their aims were little different from ours today.

Many of today's revisionist writers are not true historians in the academic sense. Very often when you analyze their writings, you find an agenda that has more to do with changing today's political landscape than with correcting the wrongs committed by our ancestors.

They tend to see our forefathers' pioneering experience in the darkest terms. They see Granddad and Great-Granddad as villainous exploiters, racists, land thieves. They somehow seem to view the pre-Columbian Americas as a paradise, where the people all lived in a happy, finely-tuned balance with Nature and with one another.

This is the *Dances With Wolves* syndrome. It was a beautiful movie, but the idyllic Indian life it presented was glorified beyond reality.

Patricia Limerick has written that the westward movement could more properly be labeled the *legacy of conquest*. My argument is not with the truth of that statement but with the inference that it was somehow peculiar to this continent, to our forefathers. That title could as properly be used for the history of all mankind. It has been the history of the world.

Man has never been a gentle creature. Ever since he first climbed out of a cave and learned to pick up a stone or a club to hit somebody with it, his history has been one of aggression, of defense, of conquest.

I do not wish to belittle the Indian or minimize the calamities that befell him, the destruction of his culture, the taking of his lands. But I believe we should recognize that the Europeans did not introduce aggression and conquest to this continent. It was here long before they came. It was here when their own ancestors were drawing charcoal pictures in European caves and learning to hammer crude implements out of bronze. Though we have no record, it probably came over on the Siberian land bridge when one group of hunters tried to beat another out of a slain mammoth.

Certainly as far back as native American legends reach, there had been recurring intertribal warfare. Hunting grounds changed hands time after time as the strong overran the weak. The carnage was sometimes unspeakable in its horror, long before Columbus ever waded ashore from his landing boat.

We need only look at the last two hundred years in Central and West Texas, at the shifts in dominance as the Apaches overran earlier tribes and as the Comanches later overran the Apaches.

Great civilizations arose to the south of us: Aztec, Mayan, Toltec. But they were built on a sea of blood—on warfare, brutal conquest, enslavement and massive human sacrifice.

The revisionists would try to tell us that our European ancestors introduced racism to these shores. But it was already here. Most Indian tribes did not recognize other tribes as being of the same race, or as being their equals.

Tribe fought against tribe for no better reason than racial prejudice. To a Cheyenne, a Crow was fair game simply because he was Crow, and Crows killed Cheyennes for the same reason. Pawnees fought the Sioux and the Cheyenne, and the Blackfeet fought just about everybody. These tribes brutally slaughtered each others's men, women and children, sometimes over hunting rights but just as often over the simple fact that they were different, and therefore inferior, and therefore fair targets.

Today's politically-correct revisionists would call that attitude racism—but only when the "wrong" people have it.

Let's talk about conquest. Consider the Comanches. They were originally a small, weak offshoot of the Shoshones, living a hand-to-mouth existence in the Rockies. There were often harshly put-upon by the stronger tribes around them. Then, somewhere around the mid 1600s, they acquired the horse and became almost overnight the most fearsome horseback warriors on the plains. Within fifty years they had swept down from the eastern Rocky

Mountains across the lower and rolling plains. They drove out or annihilated everyone who attempted to stand in their way, and they dominated the entire region from the Arkansas River to the Texas hill country.

Do you suppose they ever sat around the council fire discussing the prior rights of the tribes they dispossessed? Do you suppose they ever had historical revisionists telling them what a terrible thing it had been to drive out the Apaches, who in an earlier time had driven out the prior inhabitants?

Certainly, many of our earlier writers wrapped a false aura of glory and adventure around the exploits of our pioneer forebears. But today's politically correct revisionists propound a false myth of their own: that before the Europeans came, life on this continent was somehow an idyllic Garden of Eden. That is a pleasant little fable more in keeping with Aesop than with history.

Very few of the original Americans lived in contentment and plenty. They lived on the edge, especially in northern climates where winter was an implacable enemy. Starvation was a constant specter, lurking around the camps like hungry wolves. At best, farming was at a subsistence level, and a crop failure spelled famine. Hunting was difficult, especially before Europeans brought the horse and gave the Indians a new speed and mobility to run down the buffalo and other large game.

Even after they had the horse, northern tribes often found winter incredibly harsh. Among some of them, February was known as The Moon That the Ponies Starve. People sometimes starved, too. In some tribes, the old and infirm were cast out to freeze or starve so there might be food and shelter enough for the rest.

The Indian has been called the original conservationist, acutely aware of Nature's fine balance, careful never to disturb it. The fact is that the Indian was not averse to exploiting Nature within the limits of his technology. He used fire to manipulate the movement of game. In the horse age, his huge horse herds trampled out the grass and forced frequent moves of the camp.

Like most other people in the world, he was willing to compromise his environment to improve his life, and in the interests of commerce.

Anthropologists say that many animal species were annihilated by human hunting long before the

Europeans found this continent. And when the Indians were introduced to the wonders of European trade goods, they made deep inroads into the northern buffalo herds and the beaver streams, seeking buffalo robes and beaver pelts to sell at the white men's trading posts.

We have condemned white hide hunters for decimating the great buffalo herds, wasting the meat to obtain hides that might sell for two or three dollars apiece. Yet before they acquired the horse, Indians often drove large herds of buffalo off cliffs, killing far more than they could process before the meat spoiled.

As for living in harmony with their fellow man, this was never the case. Among most of the Western tribes, at least, warfare was a way of life. The principal duties of the adult male were usually tied directly to hunting and warfare. Only through these could a young man obtain honor and respect in the eyes of his tribe.

An old Comanche chief once protested against a proposal for peace with the Utes and other tribes he had been fighting. He said the Comanche could not live without war. Without war, the men would grow weak and effeminate.

Small tribes were always at the mercy of the larger, stronger and more warlike. Long before the white man came, the Iroquois were the terror of the weaker peoples in the Northeast. The Cherokees dominated the Southeast. The Navajos were feared and hated by all those tribes which neighbored them in the Southwest.

Have you ever wondered why the invading white man always seemed to find allies among certain Indian tribes, usually the weaker ones that had long suffered at the hands of stronger enemies?

Cortez with a relatively small band of Spanish soldiers conquered the mighty Aztec nation. In part, this was due to his superior armament. But in no small part, it was because so many non-Aztec people joined him to take revenge upon those who had for so long robbed, enslaved and slaughtered them.

There was no idyllic existence—not in Europe, not in Asia, and not in the Americas. The European invasion did not introduce conquest and subjugation to this continent. That had been here for eons. The Europeans simply were the latest in a long line of conquerors, more numerous and better armed. Prejudice had already been here, too. They simply put a different face on it.

To many Euroamericans, the Indians were savages who must either be converted to the white man's road or be exterminated. In any event, they were not to be allowed to stand in the way of the white man's claim to the land, for it was regarded as Manifest Destiny that he carry his European-derived civilization from sea to sea.

Today we recognize that Euroamerican intolerance for what it was and, to some degree, still is. Yet, that same type of intolerance already existed here.

It is not fair to judge people of the past by today's standards. They were products of their times, their environments. Can we condemn the intolerance of our European forebears without also judging the intolerance of those who preceded them here? Can we condemn their conquests without also judging the conquests of their predecessors?

We should try to see the situation through their eyes, and if we cannot fully justify what they did, perhaps we can at least understand them better. During the westward expansion, white settlers were in more-or-less constant warfare with Indians over possession of the land. Many of these Indians were relative newcomers themselves. Most of those we regard as plains tribes had moved out permanently onto the open plains only after they acquired the horse.

Blood was spilled freely on both sides, often under the most terrible circumstances. It is easy, looking back from the safe vantage point of a hundred years and more, to say that Granddad should have been more understanding. But he had seen friends and relatives killed by arrows, knives, tomahawks and bullets. Under those circumstances, how understanding would *we* be?

A common argument at the time for dispossessing the Indians was that there were so few of them, relatively speaking, and they were spread out over such a huge land area. The Euroamericans said it was unfair for so few to claim so much land.

Much the same argument is made today by political activists who call for a more even distribution of the wealth—everybody else's wealth, anyway. Some of these political activists are the same revisionists who condemn our forebears for having had a similar attitude toward someone else's land.

As a people today we have become much more ecology-minded than our ancestors, and I applaud this. However, to understand our forebears we have to recognize the way they thought. The prevailing sentiment was that the wilderness had to be "tamed" and brought into constructive use for the largest number.

Thoreau's love affair with Walden Pond was ahead of its time. Most people of his day were more inclined to agree with Stephen F. Austin, the father of Texas, that the forests must be cleared and the prairie broken to the plow. Nature was an adversary to be overcome. They would have understood the missionary character in *The African Queen* when she said, "Nature is what we are put here to rise above."

Many revisionists throw the word *greed* around like a weapon when they apply it to Granddad. Everything he did, they ascribe to his "greed."

But most of our forebears were just doing the best they knew how to make a living. Most of them did not have much by the standards of their own time, much less by the standards of ours. How can we sit in our air-conditioned offices and homes, often as not with two air-polluting cars parked in the garage, a refrigerator filled with over-rich, over-packaged food from the local supermarket, and call Granddad greedy because he wanted a hundred and sixty acres to call his own—because he wanted to shelter his family in a box cabin or a sod house and to buy his kids a new pair of shoes every year or two?

The early farmer and rancher have been blamed much in recent years for damage to the environment. *Life* magazine published a special Wild West issue which took this tack. It reprinted a famous old Dust Bowl photograph of a farmer and his two sons hurrying to get in out of a 1930s duster. The caption spoke of "greedy, ignorant farmers" despoiling the land.

If the miserable frame shack to which they were running for refuge was an example of farmer "greed," I don't know what you would call the houses in which most of us live.

Unfortunately, our forebears did do a great deal of damage to their environment. I believe most of it was due much less to greed than to lack of understanding of that environment and its limitations. Most of the first settlers came here from the East, or from Europe. They were used to a higher level of rainfall, a higher level of production.

They tried to apply their previous experience in a land where much of it did not suit the realities, especially west of the 98th meridian. The farmers farmed the best they knew how. Cattlemen looked out upon a vast open rangeland which had been vacated by the buffalo and could not visualize its limitations. Basing their judgment on past experience, they badly overestimated its carrying capacity.

The damage was not apparent overnight. It was cumulative, in many cases compounding in increments so slow that it was not noticed during one man's lifetime. A range that has developed over thousands of years is not destroyed overnight, nor can it be restored overnight. When the grass became short, it was easy to assume that this was because there had been less rainfall than last year. It was easy to say that it would be better next year. Often it was, or appeared to be.

The Dust Bowl days of the 1930s and the long drought of the 1950s taught some hard lessons in conservation. As a group, today's farmers and ranchers are doing a much better job than their forebears. But it was not greed that caused most of their forebears' mistakes. It was that they had no measuring stick to go by. They were doing the best they knew how in a new environment, and trying to survive.

Today's farmers and ranchers are doing a great deal to make up for the past. They have healed many of the scars of Dust Bowl days. And the really knowledgeable range specialists—as contrasted to some self-appointed, self-anointed urban "ecologists"—will tell you that most Western ranges are in better condition today than they have been since at least the early part of the twentieth century.

This runs counter to what some of the eco-extremists will tell you, but most of them live in urban areas which they and their neighbors have forever blighted, and they couldn't tell sideoats grama from burro grass.

Today's generational chauvinists are saying between the lines, "Isn't it wonderful how enlightened I turned out to be, especially when my ancestors were so rotten?" Or, if not *my* ancestors, certainly *yours*.

I do not claim that Granddad was blameless. But I contend that it is hypocritical to condemn him unless we are willing to shoulder our own share of the blame for the mess our country and our world are in today.

Mankind does not seem to have learned much except for an improvement in his technology. Today he can kill a lot more people at one time.

Racial, religious and tribal prejudices are world-wide. They have been with us since the dawn of man. Look at Yugoslavia, at the Middle East, at the many African countries struggling with internal warfare, black against black. They are not just a curse of the white American, or our Euroamerican ancestors.

But if you listen to the generational chauvinists, to the politically correct, you would think it all began with Granddad, that he was the serpent who spoiled the Garden of Eden.